WE HAVE RUINED MORE,
WASTED MORE, TRAMPLED ON
MORE THAN ANY CIVILIZATION
THE WORLD HAS EVER SEEN—
IN A SHORTER TIME TOO.

—FRANK LLOYD WRIGHT

LECTURE TO STUDENTS, 1950

FRANK LLOYD WRIGHT'S
LOST BUILDINGS

▦ CARLA LIND ▦

AN ARCHETYPE PRESS BOOK

POMEGRANATE ARTBOOKS, SAN FRANCISCO

© 1994 Archetype Press, Inc.

Text © 1994 Carla Lind

All rights reserved. No part of this book may be reproduced or transmitted in any form or by any means, electronic or mechanical, including photocopying, recording, or by any information storage and retrieval system, without permission in writing from the publisher.

The writings of Frank Lloyd Wright are copyright © 1994 The Frank Lloyd Wright Foundation. All rights reserved.

Library of Congress Cataloging-in-Publication Data

Lind, Carla.

Frank Lloyd Wright's lost buildings / Carla Lind.

    p.   cm.

"An Archetype Press book."

Includes bibliographical references.

ISBN 1-56640-999-3

1. Wright, Frank Lloyd, 1867–1959 — Criticism and interpretation. 2. Lost architecture — United States. I. Title.

NA737.W7L53 1994   94-7935

720'.92–dc20   CIP

Published by Pomegranate Artbooks
Box 6099, Rohnert Park,
California 94927-6099

Produced by Archetype Press, Inc.
Washington, D.C.

Project Director: Diane Maddex
Designer: Robert L. Wiser

10 9 8 7 6 5 4 3
Printed in Singapore

Opening photographs: Page 1: Frank Lloyd Wright in 1953 with a photograph of his Larkin Administration Building. Page 2: The Husser house dining room set, some of Wright's earliest furnishings.

CONTENTS

FRANK LLOYD WRIGHT, THE MOST prolific and revolutionary American architect of the twentieth century, designed nearly five hundred completed structures during his seventy-year career. Countless books and articles have been written about his contributions. Lectures and exhibits have proclaimed his importance for nearly a century. And each year hundreds of thousands of tourists visit more than fifty Wright sites that are open to the public. Despite this public acclaim, about one hundred of Frank Lloyd Wright's buildings—one of every five built—have been destroyed.

The actual number of buildings lost depends on how the count is made: some losses include multiple cottages; others involve parts of buildings; several structures were rebuilt, in part at least; and evidence about the existence of several is hazy. Gone are nineteen houses, seven multiple dwellings, twenty-six recreation structures, and eight businesses. Thirty-four of the total were either remodelings, secondary outbuildings, or temporary structures.

The exact reason many were lost is also unknown,

Portions of some of Wright's lost buildings have been salvaged and relocated, including the Imperial Hotel (pages 6–7, shown before demolition) and the Little house II (opposite), whose living room is now installed at the Metropolitan Museum of Art.

but at least fifteen of the structures were meant to be temporary, two were victims of natural disasters, about thirteen burned, six were shops or offices that changed use, and the vast majority were razed for economic reasons or a change in fashion. Most of these had deteriorated considerably before their demolition.

How could works of such an acknowledged master be destroyed? Land values increase, encouraging more remunerative uses. Neighborhoods decline, causing neglect. Tastes change, leaving Wright buildings empty and their furniture sold at garage sales. Buildings recognized as revolutionary by some are considered odd by others. Economic and social cycles vary greatly during a century.

While some might dismiss these losses as insignificant, all were part of the corpus of work of an architectural genius. Their significance lay not in the size of the commission or the original cost but in their relationship to other Wright buildings, to his life, to the time, or to the work of others. How did Wright respond to a particular need? Was this the first use of that technique? What were the sources of his design?

⠿ We are the most materialistic of all modern civilizations on earth today. We are looking too much down along our own noses and so we don't see very far into the future. ⠿

Frank Lloyd Wright
"Building for the Sick"
Speech, 1949

Sprites designed by Alfonso Ianelli for Midway Gardens now stand beside tall cactus at Taliesin West.

One of Wright's earliest and most charming commissions, a boathouse overlooking Madison's Lake Mendota, was lost in 1926.

Total loss is not the only issue. Partial destruction of Wright's multifaceted designs occurs regularly. Unlike most conventional structures, Wright buildings are characterized by numerous specially designed elements, either attached or freestanding, and all of them are integral parts of the total harmonious composition. Keeping all elements together for the lifetime of a building is a supreme challenge. Rooms are remodeled, original details lost. Furniture is sold when its art value exceeds its utilitarian value. Pieces wear out or break. Art glass windows and ornament are stolen. A new owner wants a new look.

Fortunately, most of the larger lost buildings and important spaces have been well documented in photographs, drawings, and writings. But the smaller, lesser-known ones are often forgotten, particularly if they were demolished before the 1960s. Few drawings and even fewer photographs of them are available to architectural scholars. But most important, the sheer presence of all these spaces is gone forever. Like any other work of art, each lost Wright building contained valuable information that cannot be gleaned from memories alone.

Wright designed the Francis Apartments in Chicago in 1895, just two years after leaving Louis Sullivan's office, where he mastered the use of integral, geometric ornament. They were razed in 1971.

SINCE THE EARLY 1970S INCREASED awareness has been paid to the importance of preserving the legacy of Frank Lloyd Wright. Individuals, corporations, government leaders, and foundations have joined the effort to save the Wright work that survives. Some structures considered lost by many have been rescued and miraculously brought back to life with the blood, sweat, and money of new owners with different perspectives.

While the vast majority of Wright buildings are better cared for each day, many are standing in altered or deteriorated condition. The threat of demolition hangs over their roofs. Like all aging buildings, Wright's designs require conscientious maintenance and sympathetic, dedicated stewards.

Twenty-two Wright houses are now owned and operated by organizations and are for the most part being preserved. But nearly three hundred remain in private hands, as they should be, and are the responsibility of individuals and families. To provide them a network and some technical and advisory support, the Frank Lloyd Wright Building Conservancy was formed in 1990. Through it, the

As a reminder of senseless
and tragic losses, the site
where the revolutionary
Larkin Administration
Building once stood in Buffalo,
New York, remains a
parking lot. Its light court
once brightened the day for
company employees.

efforts and knowledge of one can benefit others, lighten-
ing the load a bit.

Local historic preservation ordinances, the most
effective of all preservation tools, are being passed in
communities around the country. At least 165 Wright
buildings (forty percent) are individually listed in or are in
districts that are listed in the National Register of Historic Places. While this currently offers little real protection, such public recognition is a step in the right direc-
tion. Fortunately, none has been lost in the past decade.
With continued awareness and effort, the more than four
hundred Wright buildings that remain will survive into the
next century so that future generations will be able to experience the contributions of Frank Lloyd Wright.

Wright's buildings have proven their relevance to
today's values. They are informal, environmentally sensitive, and based on a close relationship with the earth.
They represent timeless design principles and continue to
provide durable and pleasurable shelter. In a world of lim-
ited resources, good buildings like these should be trea-
sured and cared for.

HARLAN HOUSE

CHICAGO, ILLINOIS. 1892. DEMOLISHED 1963

WRIGHT'S EMPLOYER, LOUIS SULLIVAN, easily identified the Harlan house as an after-hours Wright design. While twenty-five-year-old Wright had designed nine other "bootleg" houses, this one stood out. The geometric, nature-derived ornament for which the Adler and Sullivan office was well known, combined with the freshness of the design, gave away Wright's authorship. This deception angered Sullivan and led to Wright's departure from his mentor's office.

In the Harlan house Wright previewed many of his later Prairie Style trademarks. The low, hipped roof with broad sheltering eaves, the indirect entrance, casement windows, simple wood banding, generous terraces and verandas, and pure geometry were his preference. The spacious, two-and-a-half-story home had six bedrooms, several of which opened to balconies, all reached by a carefully articulated staircase.

By 1904 the house designed for Dr. Allison Harlan was traded for another nearby. Eventually it became a nursing home and then a vacant eyesore. After a fire caused serious damage, it was demolished.

⠿ Even in the 1950s, without the vertical members of its balcony, and in a naked, dilapidated state, the house retained an unusual sense of presence and dignity. ⠿

Werner Seligmann
Frank Lloyd Wright: A Primer on Architectural Principles, 1991

The balcony's richly textured pattern of fret-sawn leaf forms, circles, and ellipses was similar to those on Sullivan buildings. More Sullivanesque pattern adorned the newel post, and a panel of wood slats screened the stair at the entrance—Wright's earliest use of this technique.

LAKE MENDOTA BOATHOUSE

MADISON, WISCONSIN. 1893. DEMOLISHED 1926

WHEN THE MADISON IMPROVEMENT Association held a competition for boathouses on lakes Mendota and Monona, Wright submitted the winning designs. Because of the poor economy, only the smaller one, on the steep south shore of Lake Mendota, was built. It cost $3,100.

The picturesque, Shingle Style structure, symmetrical in plan, was entered from the street, where it appeared to be a one-story building. A curved arcade connected two pavilions suitable for gazing at the lake and watching the races. The boathouse, in fact, rose thirty-two feet from the lake to the top of the roofs. Below was a narrow arched harbor with a sheltered place for getting on and off boats and a curved boat storage area for twenty-eight boats that could be moved with a crane.

While the cream, red, and brown shingle-wrapped forms were reminiscent of the work of Wright's former employer, Joseph Lyman Silsbee, the curved shape and arcade show Sullivan's influence. Wright also owed a debt to his boyhood friend Robie Lamp, a boating enthusiast who probably served as his link to this project.

The broad eaves and low, pitched roof became Wright's signature in his later houses. Just thirty-three years after it was built, the boathouse was shabby and considered a nuisance to maintain on valuable land. When it was dismantled, people mourned the reduction in boat storage space more than the loss of a Wright building.

FRANCISCO TERRACE APARTMENTS

The two-story brick and stone building had forty-five units, each with its own entrance, wrapped around a central, rectangular garden court. The apartments, first known as "Honeymoon Court," were nicer than many available at twice the cost.

WRIGHT'S INTEREST IN MODERATELY priced housing began early in his career with designs for three apartment complexes on Chicago's near west side: the Francis, Waller, and Francisco Terrace buildings. The latter two were commissioned by a prominent patron of the young architect, real estate developer Edward Waller, Jr., a River Forest resident for whom Wright extensively remodeled a house (also now demolished).

Francisco Terrace was a statement of pure, utilitarian simplicity whose primary ornament was the Sullivanesque terra cotta around the arched entrance to the courtyard and on the corner stair towers. Wright's use of integral ornament, exemplified in the careful manipulation of the masonry materials, gave this low-cost housing a sense of style and dignity without extravagance.

After eight decades of hard use, the building had deteriorated and was demolished. Portions were salvaged, including the graceful entry arch. It was granted a second life in 1977 when it was incorporated into the design of a new apartment complex of similar appearance in Oak Park, Illinois. The original site remains empty.

RIVER FOREST GOLF CLUB

[The River Forest Golf Club was] "not a mere Opus I, but a First Symphony. If the essential character of its construction and design, so closely integrated as to be inseparable, can be understood, almost all the work of the first decade of Wright's maturity will fall into place.
Henry-Russell Hitchcock
In the Nature of Materials,
1942

The club's enlargement added two chimneys to the original massive masonry one that anchored the composition, whose spaciousness extended to the outside terraces.

ONE OF WRIGHT'S MOST PIVOTAL early works had a brief and unsettled life. The River Forest Golf Club was built on open land owned by real estate investor E. A. Cummings. The original board-and-batten front wing had many features identified with Wright's later Prairie Style houses. The emphasis was clearly horizontal with low, hipped roofs and continuous bands of windows with wood mullions. Large urns marked the front entrance. After three years it was compatibly enlarged, creating a symmetrical plan with an octagonal, double fireplace lounge at the center. The dining room was on one side of the foyer and lockers on the other.

By 1905 the valuable land was subdivided and the club moved farther west. Attempts to sell the building failed, so it was razed. A portion of the land was donated to the River Forest Tennis Club, which in 1906 commissioned Wright (with Charles White and Vernon Watson) to design a building for it. This was moved in 1920, when the land was sold. Yet another Wright-designed building stood briefly on the land when Cummings built his real estate office there in 1908. That too was demolished.

HUSSER HOUSE

⠿ Husser's plan, as well as its presentation technique, is that of monumental *public* construction . . . implying [Wright's] new realization that the most truly American monument was the freestanding, suburban, single-family house. ⠿

Patrick Pinnell
Frank Lloyd Wright: A Primer on Architectural Principles, 1991

Wright called for "exterior walls faced with yellow Roman brick. Horizontal joints wide and raked out to emphasize the horizontal grain. Vertical joints stopped flush with the mortar the color of the bricks."

FOR A NARROW LOT OVERLOOKING Lake Michigan on Chicago's north side, Wright designed a lavish house for the Hussers that is seen as a bridge to his later work. To maximize the panoramic views, the main living areas were placed on the second floor. The exuberant, cruciform plan was decidedly horizontal in feeling, with Sullivanesque ornament, arches, and massing. The sheltered, indirect entrance from the porte-cochère led upstairs to the expansive, uniquely open living and dining rooms, each reaching outside with a polygonal bay.

One can envision the golden design from Wright's hand-lettered description on the presentation drawings: "Stone trimming, terra cotta capitals, frieze in stucco relief, soffits plain in plaster. . . . Interior walls of lower entrance and principal rooms lined with slender Roman bricks, light tan in color carrying gold insertion and inlaid bands of olive oak, Plaster dead gold." More gold appeared in a wisteria fireplace mosaic by Ostertag and Giannini.

Eventually, other buildings rose around the house, dwarfing it and blocking its precious view of the lake. Soon it was razed to make way for an apartment building.

LARKIN ADMINISTRATION BUILDING

BUFFALO, NEW YORK. 1903. DEMOLISHED 1950

DARWIN MARTIN, ONE OF WRIGHT'S most loyal supporters, commissioned him at the height of Buffalo's industrial boom to design the headquarters for the Larkin Company, a soap manufacturer and a prosperous mail-order company. The site was in a noisy, dirty manufacturing area. Wright responded with a five-story dark red brick building with a three-story annex that turned inward. It was a successful collaboration between a sensitive client and a progressive architect.

An efficient, humane working environment was the goal, and the innovations were numerous. From the cooling system to the hermetically sealed glass windows, wall-hung toilets, and swing-out desk chairs, it was revolutionary. The roof was paved with brick as a patio for employees. The upper level had a branch library as well as a bakery, a kitchen, classrooms, dining rooms, and a conservatory.

Once the original executives were gone, the business struggled, remodeling the building as a department store in 1939 and then selling it in 1943. The city got it in 1945 and after years of neglect permitted its demolition. The lot still stands empty.

The Larkin Building was the first emphatic protest in architecture—yes—it was the first emphatic outstanding protestant against the tide of meaningless elaboration sweeping the United States....

Frank Lloyd Wright
An Autobiography, 1932

Inside the Larkin Company's assertive walls (opposite), employees worked in a sky-lighted atrium ringed by cream-colored brick balconies (page 30). Geometric-patterned piers and sphere-within-a-square lights joined metal furniture (page 31) in Wrightian harmony.

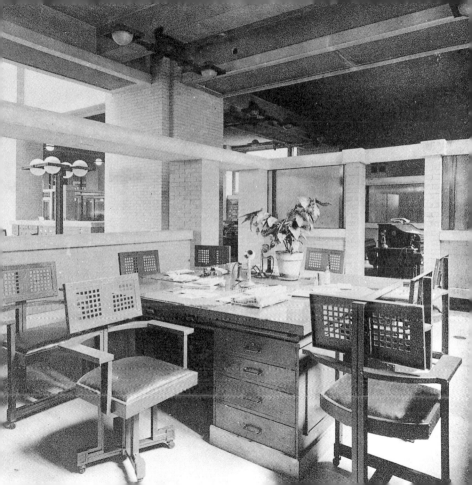

STEFFENS HOUSE

CHICAGO, ILLINOIS. 1909. DEMOLISHED 1963

CROWNING A BLUFF OVERLOOKING Lake Michigan, the Steffens house was a small but mature Prairie Style design with a two-story window wall and a generous porch. The cream-colored stucco residence included many of Wright's favorite features: low, hipped roofs, broad cantilevered overhangs, an indirect entrance, and a cruciform plan. Similar to the Isabel Roberts house, with its balconied living room, two-story core, and one-story outstretched arms, it had a unique floor plan. The staircase upstairs was on the opposite side of the living room from the stairs into the house. The living and dining rooms were on either side of the fireplace core, with screens partially concealing and then revealing new spaces.

Oscar Steffens, a businessman, chose his lot on Sheridan Road in the growing Birchwood section, but commercial development soon changed the area. He sold out in 1912 to Otto Bach, the brother of a future Wright client. By 1930 the house had been converted into a restaurant. At the time of its demolition, it was abandoned and covered with gray asbestos shingles and red trim. An apartment building stands in its place.

Geometric art glass windows mimicked the view: a golden sun at the top with diagonal blue and white shapes recalling the wind and the waves. This was one of the last houses Wright designed before he left for Europe.

LITTLE HOUSE II (NORTHOME)

WAYZATA, MINNESOTA. 1912–14. DEMOLISHED 1972

THE LITTLES WERE A PROSPEROUS family who, like Wright, were greatly interested in music. In 1903 Wright designed a Prairie Style house for them in Peoria, Illinois. When they moved to Minneapolis, they asked Wright to design them a new home—this time on a large, wooded lakeside lot. It had a faltering birth, a senseless death, and a partial reincarnation.

Francis and Mary Little approached Wright about the country house in 1908 but agreed to wait while he straightened out his personal life. It would be six years before they moved in. One of his last houses to be called Prairie Style, Northome was finally constructed on the gentle hills adjoining Lake Minnetonka. The living room, which doubled as a concert hall, was nearly fifty feet long and had a separate entrance.

In 1972, after the family failed to get approval for a second home on the site, they decided to demolish the house. Alerted to the imminent demise of Wright's work, the Metropolitan Museum of Art documented it, saved some parts, sold several rooms to others, and reconstructed the living room in its American Wing.

The library (opposite) was obtained and installed by the Allentown Museum of Art. In the house, new Wright designs had supplemented furniture from the Littles' Peoria house.

On its original site (pages 36–37), dozens of art glass panels opened the space and framed rather than competed with views of the woods and the lake— inviting music, nature, and well-composed architecture to interact.

MIDWAY GARDENS

CHICAGO, ILLINOIS. 1913-14. DEMOLISHED 1929

Like musical notes, geometric shapes were composed into visual melodies, movements, and symphonies (opposite).

A model (below) shows the multitiered, outdoor Summer Garden focused on the orchestra shell. At the other end was the Winter Garden, for dancing, dining, and music in bad weather. Adjoining were the Tavern and Midway Garden Club, for more intimate gatherings.

WRIGHT'S RECENT TRIP TO EUROPE enabled him to share the vision of Edward Waller, Jr., for a first-rate outdoor concert garden on Chicago's south side. Together they created an entertainment center that integrated visual and performing arts within an architectural masterpiece—a luscious, sensual experience.

Midway's artistic team included Alfonso Ianelli and Richard Bock as sculptors, three painters, and Wright's son John as the superintendent. Paul Mueller, Wright's friend from Sullivan's office, served as engineer, and prominent chefs and musicians were engaged.

Although it was enthusiastically received (17,000 patrons on one weekend), Midway Gardens was vastly underfinanced and operated for only two years. Waller sold the property to the Schoenhofen Brewery for use as a beer garden. It remained open during Prohibition, finally closing in 1928. Wright's complex was demolished in 1929 after being sold to the Sinclair Oil Company—replaced by a gas station with a car wash. Public housing now stands on the place where the renowned Anna Pavlova once danced.

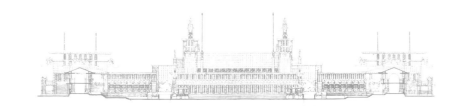

Spires of cubes rose from
concrete and brick walls
(opposite). Ianelli's sprites
surrounded the sunken garden; winged figures (left)
framed interior and exterior
facades. Murals of circles bub-
bled in the Tavern (page 42),
while triangles danced in the
art glass windows. In addition
to seven hundred seats near
the stage, countless tables
and chairs filled the court
and surrounding balconies
(page 43). Wright's furniture
was never executed, but
his lamps and tableware en-
hanced the dining experience.

IMPERIAL HOTEL

TOKYO, JAPAN. 1915-19. DEMOLISHED 1968

THE IMPERIAL HOTEL COMMISSION followed closely on the heels of Midway Gardens and shared its exuberance and exotic appearance. The four-story structure was built primarily of textured brick (tan outside, brown with golden mortar joints inside) and Oya, a light lava stone that was easily cut or carved. Concrete, wood, copper, and terra cotta tiles also were used. Surfaces were textured with molded or carved geometric forms—an ultimate example of integral ornament.

Wright and Paul Mueller engineered a cantilevered, reinforced concrete foundation that floated on piers in the unstable soil. The building's genius was revealed in some two hundred rooms, a theater and banquet hall, a promenade, a two-story dining room, and a three-story lobby with bar, each promising surprises.

The hotel miraculously survived an earthquake in 1923 and the bombings of World War II but not the pressure of rising land values. In 1967 the Japanese were caught by surprise at the proposed demolition. The hotel was torn down, but a portion   the entrance, lobby, and pool—was rebuilt at the Meija-Mura outdoor museum.

⊞ . . . it was my desire to help Japan make the transition from wood to masonry and from her knees to her feet without too great loss of her own great accomplishments in civilization. ⊞

Frank Lloyd Wright
An Autobiography, 1932

Imaginative furnishings (opposite and page 46) reflected the shapes of the building; the low pitch of the ceiling was repeated in hexagonal chair backs and mural designs. Pools, gardens (page 47), urns, grilles, carpets, china, and silver service were all woven into the three-dimensional tapestry.

OCATILLA CAMP

CHANDLER, ARIZONA. 1928. DEMOLISHED 1930

Although the quarters at his desert camp were temporary (opposite), Wright furnished them thoughtfully with Indian textiles and even a grand piano.

WHEN ALEXANDER CHANDLER APPROACHED Wright in 1928 about designing a resort called San Marcos in the Desert, he responded with enthusiasm. These were quiet times in Wright's office, so the promise of a big project and change of scene appealed to him. Without final confirmation, the family and draftsmen packed up and drove from Wisconsin to the Arizona desert.

Then sixty-one, Wright was inspired by the desert's new set of building materials, forms, colors, and quality of light. His first challenge was to create some temporary housing for his entourage. The result was Ocatilla: simple, geometric, tentlike abstractions whose wood-battened walls crept along the desert floor. White canvas roofs stretched over triangular wood frames above them, repeating the angles of the mountains.

Wright found conditions in Arizona more comfortable than Wisconsin in the winter. The cabins (pages 50–51), with their triangular canvas gables painted red, were inexpensively built by the apprentices in six weeks.

When funding for the resort fell through, the camp was abandoned and gradually fell apart. But it provided the inspiration for Taliesin West in concept and form. Ten years later the Taliesin Fellowship moved into its new winter headquarters in the desert near Scottsdale, Arizona. In a sense, Ocatilla was its preliminary sketch.

PAUSON HOUSE

ROSE PAUSON AND HER SISTER WERE potters and weavers from a prominent San Francisco family. The home Wright designed for them was born of the desert and enriched by their personal sense of style. It was built on a knoll near the Arizona Biltmore Hotel, where the sisters had vacationed for years.

Like an excavated temple from an earlier civilization, the house had lapped wood over dark red desert stone walls that were canted like the surrounding mountains. It was handcrafted like a piece of cabinetry, each board specially milled six times. The in-line plan of the Usonian design placed the bedrooms upstairs and the living-dining area, kitchen, and servants' quarters below. Opened with glass on two sides, the house's other facades were closed—their cool stone walls offering protection from the desert heat and wind.

On a cold evening just two years after its creation, the house burned to the ground when sparks from the fireplace ignited the handwoven curtains. All that remained was the massive stone chimney and foundation. For years this relic stood as a landmark and gathering place.

The two-story living room had twelve-foot-high windows on either side (opposite) and joined with one of several terraces to double its size.

The technique used for laying stone in forms and then infilling with concrete (page 54) was one Wright had developed at Taliesin West— an organic response to the nature of the site. In 1979 the ruins (page 55) were moved so that a road could be built.

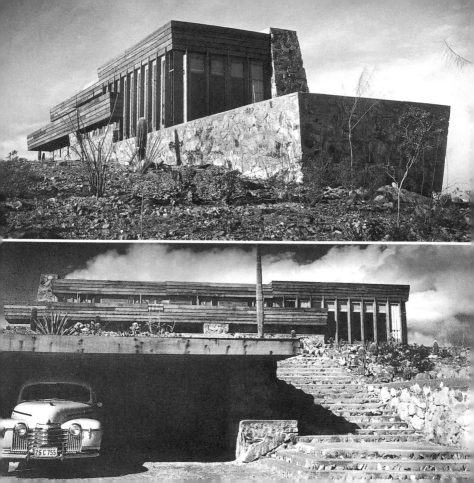

Hitchcock, Henry-Russell. *In the Nature of Materials: The Buildings of Frank Lloyd Wright, 1887–1941*. 1942. Reprint. New York: Da Capo Press, 1969.

James, Cary. *Frank Lloyd Wright's Imperial Hotel*. New York: Dover Publications, 1988.

Manson, Grant Carpenter. *Frank Lloyd Wright to 1910: The First Golden Age*. New York: Van Nostrand Reinhold, 1958.

Quinan, Jack. *Frank Lloyd Wright's Larkin Building: Myth and Fact*. Architectural History Foundation. Cambridge: MIT Press, 1987.

Wright, Frank Lloyd. *Drawings and Plans of Frank Lloyd Wright: The Early Period (1893–1909)*. 1910. Reprint. New York: Dover Publications, 1983.

———. *The Early Work of Frank Lloyd Wright: The "Ausgeführte Bauten" of 1911*. Reprint. New York: Dover Publications, 1982.

———. *Frank Lloyd Wright: The Complete 1925 "Wendingen" Series*. Reprint. New York: Dover Publications, 1992.

ACKNOWLEDGMENTS

The author wishes to thank the Frank Lloyd Wright Home and Studio Foundation Research Center, Oak Park Public Library, Jack Holzueter, Paul Kruty, and Tim Samuelson.

Archetype Press is grateful to Pedro E. Guerrero for his assistance with the cover illustration by Robert L. Wiser.

Illustration Sources:

Allentown Art Museum, gift of Audrey and Bernard Berman, 1972: 35 bottom (72.94)

Art Institute of Chicago, Ryerson and Burnham Libraries: 19, 32, 39, 40 bottom, 41, 42, 43 bottom; 38 (model by Richard Tickner, photo by Robert Hashimoto, 1989.48)

Ausgeführte Bauten und Entwürfe von Frank Lloyd Wright (Wasmuth, 1910): 14, 24 top, 25, 28, 30 right

Richard Bowditch: 11

Buffalo and Erie County Historical Society, Larkin Collection: 16, 29, 30 left, 31

Chicago Historical Society: 15 top left (Charles R. Childs), 15 top right (Arthur Siegel, G 1980.0024), 22 (Arthur Siegel, ICHi-20305), 43 top (J. W. Taylor, ICHi-01436)

Frank Lloyd Wright: Ausgeführte Bauten (Wasmuth, 1911): 27 top and bottom

Frank Lloyd Wright Home and Studio Foundation: 6–7 (H&S 373), 44 (H&S 381), 46 (H&S 569), 47 (H&S 374)

Pedro E. Guerrero: 1, 53, 54 top and bottom

Historical Society of Oak Park and River Forest: 23 (Gilman Lane)

Historic American Buildings Survey: 15 bottom left and right, 33, 55

Balthazar Korab Ltd.: 2 (Gary Quesada)

© Norman McGrath: 8

Metropolitan Museum of Art, courtesy Mrs. Raymond V. Stevenson: 36–37

Oak Park Public Library: 24 bottom

State Historical Society of Wisconsin: 12, 20 top and bottom, 48, 49, 50–51

Wendingen Series (Mees, 1925): 35, 40 top

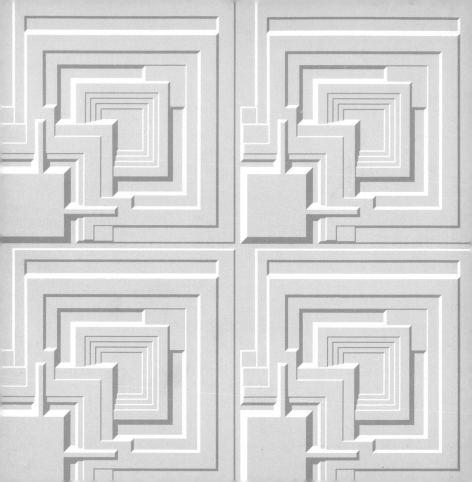